Apatosaurus

The Thunder Lizard

Dinosaur Books for Young Readers

By Enrique Fiesta
Mendon Cottage Books

JD-Biz Publishing

Read More Amazing Animal Books

Purchase at Amazon.com

Download Free Books!
http://MendonCottageBooks.com

Table of Contents

Introduction

Greetings young reader! Today we are going to take a step back in time and enter the age of the dinosaurs. The dinosaurs are an extinct species of animal that began to live on the Earth over 200 million years ago. "Extinct" means that they no longer exist. The dinosaurs are some of the most intriguing and awe-inspiring animals that have existed on our planet. The dinosaurs' colossal size, strange characteristics, and mysterious disappearance make them *inherently* worthy of study and interest. Even more than these reasons, the study of dinosaurs itself is an incredible adventure which requires thought and imagination. The study of dinosaurs helps you to appreciate just how mysterious and amazing life and nature really is. Our planet supports not only us and the animals that live today, but it even supported creatures as gigantic and strange as the dinosaurs- just think how cool that is! I hope that you bring a spirit of openness and wonder to your study of the dinosaurs, and that you come to appreciate the mystery and value of the dinosaurs.

The dinosaur we are discussing today is the Apatosaurus. The Apatosaurus was a gigantic herbivore and one of the largest land-dwelling animals to live on earth. It is well known for its gigantic neck and tail but we are not only going to learn about the dinosaur's appearance, but also its probable behavior and environment. We know what we know about the dinosaurs from a variety of sources including fossils, biology, and other scientific disciplines. Fossils are the ancient remains of the dinosaurs, the most familiar being their bones. Biological science is the study of life in general, but many scientists compare the dinosaurs to modern day animals to support their theories.

Before a talk about dinosaurs can take place it is important that we discuss the theory of evolution. Evolutionary theory supposes that all the animals we know and see today are the direct descendants of animals that existed millions of years ago. The dinosaurs and other creatures that existed millions of years ago either died out or gradually changed into different animals. For instance, birds are considered to be surviving dinosaurs because their dinosaur ancestors survived the dinosaur extinction event (we will discuss this later).

Chapter 1: Appearance

The name Apatosaurus means "deceptive lizard." This is because the first scientists who discovered the fossils believed the dinosaur was a **mosasaur**. A mosasaur is an aquatic dinosaur with flippers and a large head full of sharp teeth. When the scientists discovered it was not a mosasaur, they called the fossils deceptive. The Apatosaurus is often called Brontosaurus. Brontosaurus is a combination of two Greek words which means "thunder lizard."

The Apatosaurus was one of the largest **terrestrial herbivores** to live on earth. **Terrestrial** means "land-dwelling." An **herbivore** is an animal which eats plants in order to survive. This dinosaur belonged to a group of dinosaurs called the **sauropods**. The sauropods were long necked, long tailed dinosaurs with a thick torso, thick legs, and a small head. The Apatosaurus could grow up to a length of 90 ft. and a height of 15 ft. at the hips. The tail of the Apatosaurus was long and whip-like and could reach a length of about 50 ft. The Apatosaurus also had a very long neck and could have held its head up to 17 ft. off the ground. The Apatosaurus could reach a weight of up to 38 tons.

The Apatosaurus was a **quadruped**. A quadruped is an animal which walks on all four legs. The legs of the Apatosaurus were equipped with a long claw. The legs looked like thick, columns and they were powerful enough to support its large, heavy body.

The head of the Apatosaurus was only about 2 ft. long. Compared to the rest of its body, the head of the Apatosaurus was incredibly tiny. The brain of this dinosaur was also incredibly small. Scientists believe that the Apatosaurus had incredibly simple behavior because of its small brain size. The Apatosaurus had comb-like teeth, each tooth looking like a peg or a pencil. The Apatosaurus's nostrils were on the top of its head. Currently, scientists are unsure why the nostrils were on top of its head. The first **hypothesis** was that they lived underwater with their heads held close to the surface in order to breathe. A hypothesis is a proposed explanation for a given problem, generally based on scientific research. The fossils of the Apatosaurus were found far away from large bodies of water, so it is improbable that they lived or fed underwater.

Chapter 2: Behavior

The Apatosaurus held its head parallel to the ground and used its long neck to eat wide stretches of plants, foliage, and vegetation. It may have also used its long neck to eat the leaves of trees in forests that other dinosaurs were not able to reach.

The Apatosaurus had to have eaten a large amount of vegetation in order to stay alive. The Apatosaurus was most likely a warm-blooded animal because of its large size. The Apatosaurus would not have been able to warm its entire body using sunlight alone, so it is likely it had to have eaten a lot of food in order maintain a warm body temperature. The Apatosaurus probably spent a lot of its time grazing with its rake-like teeth. The comb-like mouth would have allowed the dinosaur to strip the foliage off branches and bushes. Some scientists believe the Apatosaurus had lips like modern mammals which would have allowed the dinosaur to pull leaves into its mouth with its lips.

The Apatosaurus most likely did not chew its food, but instead ate its food whole. Like modern birds and some mammals, the Apatosaurus swallowed stones to help break down food in its stomach. These stones are called **gastroliths**. The main food source of the Apatosaurus was probably conifer trees, but it probably ate mosses, gingkos, and ferns to supplement its primary diet.

Apatosaurus swallowed leaves and other vegetation whole, without chewing them, and had gastroliths (stomach stones) in its stomach to help digest this tough plant material.

The Apatosaurus may have travelled in herds like many modern day herbivores. The dinosaur was extremely unintelligent and moved extremely slowly. A herd would have intimidated predators.

The Apatosaurus defended itself not only by living in a herd, but also with its long-tail, sharp claws, and large size. The Apatosaurus could hold its head higher than most predators could reach, so predators were left with either the option to attack the torso or the tail. The torso was guarded by the sharp claws of the feet, while the tail itself was a deadly and powerful weapon. The dinosaur is similar to the modern day giraffe because of its long neck and ability to deliver deadly strikes to predators. The giraffe can kill a full grown lion with a single kick- just imagine what the Apatosaurus could do with its 2,000 lb legs!

Chapter 3: Environment

The Apatosaurus lived about 156-144 million years ago during the **Mesozoic Era** which began about 250 million years ago, specifically during the **Jurassic Period**. The Mesozoic Era is often divided into three periods: the Triassic, Jurassic, and Cretaceous. The dinosaurs disappeared at the end of the Cretaceous during an event called the K-Pg extinction event. The demise of the dinosaurs was probably caused by a combination of factors including meteoric impacts, climate change, and disease.

The Apatosaurus lived in Jurassic North America. The Jurassic climate was warm and moist. Some areas were arid and dry but most of the Jurassic world was lush and green. The Apatosaurus lived in bio-diverse environs and lived with many other dinosaurs. It lived with predators and other herbivores such as the Diplodocus, Allosaurus, and Stegosaurus.

The Diplodocus was another sauropod who lived alongside the Apatosaurus. The two dinosaurs are similar in size and weight and probably shared very similar behaviors.

The Allosaurus was a **therapod** who lived in the same region as the Apatosaurus. A therapod is a typically bipedal (walks on two legs) predatory dinosaur. The Allosaurus was an **apex hyperpredator** in Jurassic North America. A hyperpredator is a predator whose diet consists 70% of meat. An *apex predator* is a predator which exists at the top of its food chain. The Allosaurus grew up to 30 ft. long and up to 15ft. high. The Allosaurus would have been the primary predator of the fully grown Apatosaurs. The Apatosaurus would have had to use its long whip-like tail and long claws to defend itself from the Allosaurus.

The Stegosaurus was a quadrupedal dinosaur with plates lining its entire back; from its head to the end of its tail. The end of the Stegosaurus's tail was lined with deadly spikes. The Stegosaur used its tail to ward off predators like the Allosaurus. It is possible that Stegosaurs and Apatosaurs lived close together like modern day African mammals.

Conclusion

We have stepped back in time to look at this dinosaur, where and when it lived, and the dinosaurs it lived with. By using our imaginations and knowledge we can engage, wonder about, and appreciate the mystery and value of the dinosaurs. By learning about and appreciating what the dinosaurs are we come to appreciate our own present age and all the wonderful creatures that live today. We discover how varied and mysterious life really is- we look at animals today with a newfound appreciation and awe. Make sure you keep thinking, learning, and imagining, and *really* make sure that you never lose your sense of wonder.

Author Bio

Enrique Fiesta

I was born in Southwest Florida and I hold a degree in Latin and Greek language and literature. In addition to my principal studies, I have also studied philosophy, history, the natural sciences, and literature. In my spare time I devote the vast majority of my time to reading, writing, praying, and walking. I am currently pursuing legal studies in order to become an attorney. After I earn my law degree I intend to pursue a doctorate in philosophy, literature, and politics.

Our books are available at

1. Amazon.com

2. Barnes and Noble

3. Itunes

4. Kobo

5. Smashwords

6. Google Play Books

Download Free Books!
http://MendonCottageBooks.com

Publisher

JD-Biz Corp

P O Box 374

Mendon, Utah 84325

http://www.jd-biz.com/

www.ingramcontent.com/pod-product-compliance
Lightning Source LLC
Chambersburg PA
CBHW042240290526
45792CB00021B/959